Arthur, his Grandad, and their Magic Car.

By Michael Bolger

For Arthur -

Because you believed in the Magic Car. x

Arthur,

His Grandad

And Their

Magic Car

Once upon a time, a long, l-o-n-g time ago there lived an old man who was a rather clever magical inventor he lived in Norwich in a magical party of the City and every morning he could be found whistling away in his workshop as he invented different magical machines.

Grandad's workshop when he worked there.

This what Grandad's workshop looks like today....

No one was really interested in his machines because they were pretty stupid. His Grandson would of visit him and told Grandad how great his inventions were even though three-year old Arthur knew they were pretty rubbish! Who really wanted a machine that would blow your nose for you? What use was there for a bicycle with square wheels, or a little cart for a cat to pull around behind it?

Even Arthur's pet dragon, who was pretty useless as a fiery dragon, knew Grandad's inventions were no good.

Arthur's Dad was always keen to make sure he was safe, so whenever he left the house he had to take his dragon with him. He also had to take plenty of water because Dennis was always setting fire to things by mistake and Arthur had to put the fires out.

Dennis the Useless Dragon.

Arthur knew Grandad was quite happy inventing stuff no one wanted so he just smiled and told the old man that he thought it was really clever. Whenever he could, Arthur would take his tool kit and rush off to

Grandad's workshop to help him. The two would work together for hours until Arthur's Mum would come calling for him at bedtime.

One day Arthur collected his toolbox from home and trotted off to Grandad's workshop as usual only to find the door locked and Grandad was not whistling. Arthur stopped still and called out, "Ga-Ga? Are you there?" Arthur always called Grandad "Ga-Ga" by the way.

There was no reply so the boy called again, still nothing. Arthur was getting worried. Where could Ga-Ga be?

Then, suddenly he heard the creaky door lock turn and Grandad poked his head round the corner.

"My Boy", he whispered, "I think I've done it. I think I've invented something that everyone will want. Come in, come it quickly". The door opened a crack and Arthur slipped in.

At the back of the workshop stood a huge 'thing'. Arthur couldn't call it more than a 'thing' because it was completely covered by a huge red velvet cover.

Dennis hid behind Arthur as if the small boy could protect him and he puffed a bit of smoke and fire at the 'thing'. He really was a bit useless as a pet dragon!

"Stand there Arthur. I'll show you what I've made. I really think you're going to love it".

Arthur prepared himself to be disappointed while Grandad who had had a bad leg for a while, shuffled across to the red cover. He grabbed a corner and asked unnecessarily "Ready?"

"Yes", said Arthur, "Go for it Ga-Ga". Dennis let out a little puff of steam and hid even further behind his young master.

With a flourish, Grandad whipped away the cover and stood back. Arthur' mouth fell open and he gently kicked Dennis as he could hear the dragon sniggering.

The sight that greeted Arthur took his breath away with its 'rubbishness'. It was……. AN OLD CAR. A rubbish old car.

"Ga-Ga, you didn't invent that – someone else do. A long time ago by the look of it." Another kick for Dennis.

"Ahhh", said Grandad, "That's what you are supposed to think. Wait. Watch this."

Grandad went to the car climbed in very carefully and switched it on and started the engine. "Here comes the clever bit". With that Grandad shut the door, dramatically put some goggles on and pressed several buttons and moved levers. The car was now making odd noises – very odd noises and Arthur thought he should get his Mum so she could stop this nonsense.

Then it happened. Very slowly, the car started to rise from the ground and started to move around the workshop knocking several things over on its journey.

This time Arthur and Dennis stood with their mouths open in amazement and admiration for what they were seeing.

Then, as quickly as the demonstration had stared, it finished. The car landed at the other end of Grandad's workshop with a bump.

Grandad got out carefully and beamed broadly at Arthur. "What do you think?" For once, Arthur was 'good speechless'.

"GA-GA, IT'S BRILLIANT. Can I have a go?"

"Not yet. I haven't quite worked out how to steer it yet – but I'm nearly there. In a week we will be able to roll it out and fly it around Norwich as the two proudest inventors you'll ever meet"

Grandad's workshop....

Sadly, things were not going to work out that way. Oh, Grandad would get the steering sorted out. He even persuaded Nanna to take a few flights with him around the workshop although she was even more frightened by him driving a flying car than she was when he drove his normal car.

The problem was that the workshop was in a street in Norwich very near the market and there were lots of other inventors working near there. One, who had always been jealous of Grandad and Arthur and their family, had noticed the door slightly open Nanna had left it open because she said Grandad's workshop stunk. Nutjob, the rival had seen a test flight and knew exactly who he would go too with the information. And with his black pointy hat and pointy nose he headed off to a place called Suffolk where the King would pay him well for the information.

Norwich had a castle on a hill. You might know it. It's still there today. It's big and square and there is usually a crane next to it and the buses stop underneath it.

King Nodge's Castle

The King who lived there was a really good man. He had been 'kinging' since he was 13 years old and his name was King Nodge and everyone loved him. He had grown into a tall and kind man who was loved by the people of Norwich as much as his father had been before him.

Sadly, his Uncle, who was now King of Suffolk, hated him for sending him away twenty years earlier and it was to that same King of Suffolk who Nutjob the inventor was heading with his tale of a flying car that would make anyone loved by their people.

On Saturday morning, Grandad and Arthur were ready to roll out their flying car. They had told Nanna and Arthur's Mum and Dad (especially his Dad!) that they would be flying in the afternoon and that Arthur would NOT be in the car, even in a six-point F1 harness and wrapped in a complete roll of bubble wrap.

At 9 o'clock the rolled the car out and pushed it beside the big shop that had a bit of a slope next to it so they could get it going.

At 9 o'clock some of the King of Suffolk's soldiers were crossing from Suffolk intending to grab the car in the workshop and take it back across the border.

At 9 o'clock King Nodge was doing his exercises on top of his castle. He did them every day, never fail.

It all happened at once. Grandad and Arthur gathered speed down the road and, after a couple of bumps, took off gracefully. Grandad driving, Arthur next to him and Dennis hiding in the back.

The castle guard spotted the Suffolk Solders making their way towards Norwich.

Arthur and Grandad first past over Arthur's house and a loud beep on the horn soon had Mum and Dad and Daisy the Cat standing in the back yard. They were waving frantically, and Arthur waved back. They were actually shouting to them to "GET DOWN HERE, NOW!"

Next, they flew to Nanna and Grandad's house and Nanna was waving too. Arthur again waved back. Although Nanna was cross that they were up there she was annoyed that she wasn't up there with them and wanted a go herself.

The flying car turned to fly back to Norwich and as they did so Grandad spotted the Suffolk Soldiers. "Umm, think we have trouble coming", he said. "Dennis, grab those bags beside you and get ready to drop them. I was hoping to drop them on Nutjob's house, but no matter, I can see he's with those Suffolk Soldiers so I have an idea what's going on. They're after our car"

Dennis gripped the bags between his teeth and Grandad told him he'd tell when to release them. Arthur wanted to know what was in them. Grandad said it was a special mixture he had invented that was the smelliest stuff ever. It stuck to people and would never come off. He'd just never had a use for it before – until now, that is!

"Bombs away", shouted Grandad. Then he realised Dennis was still holding them. "YOU, DOPY THE DRAGON – LET GO!"

Dennis felt slightly hurt but let go anyway and the bags landed right on top of the soldiers. "Bulls Eye" shouted Grandad especially pleased to watch one land directly on Nutjob.

The car circled and the three watched as the soldiers were all running as fast as their smelly legs would carry them, back to Suffolk. Nutjob just stood crying in the middle of the road as Nodge's guards arrived and arrested him. They just didn't get too close. Neither did anyone else - for many years.

"Time to head home", said Grandad.

But just then the car juddered and made a clunky noise. "Oh dear. I was afraid that might happen."

"What's wrong Ga-Ga?" asked Arthur.

"It's the steering linkages I'm afraid. I had to use two beer cans and a pair of Nanna's old knickers in the end, and it looks like the elastic has broken. Hold tight. We're going down."

The car flew over the City with thousands of people cheering with no idea they were about to see a crash landing. Grandad and Arthur couldn't resist a quick wave as they passed the market. They were too fast and too high and the crash happened.

The car passed straight through two workshops and into the wall of the upstairs of Grandad's workshop. The front of the car had made it, just the back was sticking out.

"Everyone OK?" asked Grandad.

"We are" answered Arthur having checked Dennis.

The three climbed out and brushed the muck and dust off themselves and had their second big surprise of the day. There, waiting for them in Grandad's workshop, stood a beaming King Nodge.

"Fan – blooming – tastic", he shouted as he rushed towards them for a group hug. "I haven't enjoyed something so much since I was Young Nodge. Tell me Grandad, would you accept the job as Royal Magical Inventor. You could have your own big workshop in the castle and you and Arthur can work there. It's a much higher place to launch a flying car from as well!"

They all laughed until their sides ached.

"I'll need to clear this lot up first and get rid of that car", said Grandad.

"I've got a better idea", said Nodge, "Let's leave it right here so little children can come and see it for years to come".

"Brilliant! Let's do that," said Grandad. The four walked off to face the cheers of the crowds round the market.

….And to this day the magical car still sits there in the wall.

And there it is – right where Arthur and Grandad crashed it!

So, if you ever find yourself in Norwich, remember to go to the restaurant and take a look at the magic car where it crashed through the wall.

This book was written for Arthur Ratcliffe to celebrate Christmas 2023 and his 3rd birthday on 9th January 2023.

This book is the fourth in the series of King Nodge books although Nodge doesn't play much of a part himself. It's 20 years since his last adventure and he is now 33 years old. The series will continue as the friendship between Nodge and Arthur grows and their adventures will continue later in 2024.

Printed in Great Britain
by Amazon

35860364R00016